FUN WITH PHONICS

Learn to read with

Baby bug

Words by Sue Graves
Illustrations by Jan Smith

book-studio

Mum gave a present to Baby bug.

"Happy birthday," said Mum. She gave him a hug.

"Wow!" said Baby bug. He dug and he dug.

First he dug up
a big green jug.

Next he dug up an old red mug.

Then he dug up a toy pug. "Wow!" he said. "I shall hug this pug."

Just then he
saw a rug.
He gave it
a big tug.

Suddenly out came the rug.

"Where is Baby bug?" said Mum with a shrug.

"Help!"

The end